TWO BOOKS

JOHN ASH was born in Manchester in 1948 and read English at the University of Birmingham. He has been the recipient of both a Guggenheim Fellowship and the Whiting Foundation Award. His Carcanet books include *The Goodbyes* (Poetry Book Society Choice, 1982), *The Branching Stairs* (1984), *Disbelief* (Poetry Book Society Choice, 1987) and *The Burnt Pages* (1991).

Also by John Ash from Carcanet

The Goodbyes
The Branching Stairs
Disbelief
The Burnt Pages
Selected Poems

JOHN ASH

Two Books

The Anatolikon / To the City

CARCANET

First published in Great Britain in 2002 by
Carcanet Press Limited
4th Floor, Conavon Court
12-16 Blackfriars Street
Manchester M3 5BQ

A CIP catalogue record for this book
is available from the British Library
ISBN 1 85754 560 5

The publisher acknowledges financial assistance
from the Arts Council of England

Set in Ehrhardt by Bryan Williamson, Frome
Printed and bound in England by SRP Ltd, Exeter

Contents

THE ANATOLIKON

TO THE CITY

Part I

Part II

Part III

The Anatolikon

They said: 'Why do you want to go to that place? There is
    nothing to see.'
And I said: 'But I like its name. It means "opium" and
    "fortress".
It has something to do with the colours blue and red . . .' So,
In a dusty square with a flower garden and a nearly extinct
    fountain
I took a bus which passed through many bus stations
(In one of which I examined displays of very ugly meerschaum
    pipes)
And Andrew came with me to keep a photographic record
Of everything that was to be seen and not seen along the way.
In Afyon I admired the baroque frames of the restaurant
    mirrors,
The dazzling aprons of the waiters, and the colours of the
    houses. A rat
Ran up the steps from the garden, then paused as if uncertain
    what to do.
We met two young salesmen from Usak who sang for us on
    the summit
Of the fortress rock, which was black but patterned with
    brilliant lichens.
We were sad to discover that all the kilims had been stolen
    from the mosque.
We went south through fields of roses, their perfume
    smothering the valleys,
Rising up in gusts towards peaks like broken knives. The heat
Grew more intense. The trees died out and returned. It was
    early June.
All through the spring it had rained, and flowers covered
    the plateau.
The stone lions of Phrygia roared and leapt. Rainstorms
    filled the cisterns

In the City of Midas. The road was imperial and straight.
My eyes grew tired with looking. In the distance I saw an
enormous cloud,
Which turned out to be the sunlit snows of a mountain too high
and too broad
For the mind to take in. On its lower slopes, a score of
murdered princes
Lay buried in tombs painted with hyacinths and quince
flowers.
A melody by Gluck came over the car radio, and at once the
column shafts
Appeared among the rocks. A donkey brayed in the sanctuary
of a temple.
Dwarf pines like blue stubble covered the slopes, and birds
flew off at the edge of the road,
And still I kept looking for something that was not there amid
so much that was.
Women, dressed as if for a wedding, rode through fields of
white and purple poppies.
In the evenings a cold breeze blew down from the north of
the lake,
And suddenly the water turned the colour of slate,
And somewhere in those hills, beyond the little fort of
Myriocephalon,
In a narrow valley, in the midst of a sandstorm, the Emperor
Manuel was defeated,
And it was said of him that, 'Never thereafter did he exhibit
His former gaiety of spirit, or show himself joyful before his
people
No matter how much they entreated him.' On the island of
Nis,
A young man named Mustafa addressed me in four languages,
And in the fourth (English) offered to lend me his father's
car
For a few days of sightseeing in the mountains. In the
garden

Of a shuttered house, beneath a tangle of old vines, a fishing-
boat
Lay on its side, its wood so weathered it seemed only the
memory of a boat.
The road looped north, then south, before turning east into a
valley sparsely patched with fields.
The old man sold me saffron. The laughter of Mrs Bilir was
as pretty as birdsong.
At Belisirma a woman with the bearing of an empress strode
across a bridge.
In the patio-restaurant of Mrs Uzun, the Australians drank
red wine
Followed by raki, and next day nothing was heard from them.
By the Well of the Pomegranates I are grilled mullet and
arugula.
In the Cave of Heaven the lights failed. On a promontory
where sand dunes
Had covered a city, I met a schoolteacher who was reading
Herodotus.
He asked me what I was looking for in the ruins so late in the day,
And I could not answer him. Turtles copulated in a damp
hollow nearby.
Dogs kept me company, cats greeted me. The ground was
starred with crocuses.
The sea was calm. A fire was lit on the beach, and the young
men leapt through the flames.
And still the women rode out to the fields dressed in
turquoise and violet.
The cars paraded through the town, horns blazing, and in the
first car sat a boy
Dressed like a prince in a cap and cape of midnight blue
strewn with stars.
The twins ran towards me holding flowers. The village was
poor and the catch reduced —
Ferocious pike twitched in baskets on the quay and a stork
folded its wings.

But what was I looking for? I had walked through a mountain
And emerged on a ledge hundreds of feet above the town
square.
In circular chambers I had seen doors like gigantic mill-
stones thrown on their sides.
I had gone down eight storeys into the earth, and what had I
brought back?
Only the words of some old songs, badly translated:
Young Constantine went to war . . . or *I built strong walls.*
*I made doors of iron to keep out death but death was there
beside me.*
The walls of Iznik were four miles long. The beautiful tiles
were no longer made.
A chestnut stallion pranced nervously by the Roman theatre.
In the tomb there were peacocks that reached towards a vase
that had vanished,
And poplars rustled where a spring flowed across the track
In the shadow of a tower. In the garden of the Pine Tree Hotel
An acanthus capital supported a can of geraniums,
And the young waiters asked us for news of America.
A party of women moved along the esplanade, and the one
who led them
Tapped her fingers on a small drum. The church that was
called red
Lay isolated in a lake of white flowers, close to a village of
caves,
And a lizard the colour of an Ottoman emerald ran across
the stones.
At last I entered a broad and pleasant valley and there I
found a tomb
Like a pleasure pavilion, and a monastery surrounded by
apple trees
Where a yellow vine curled across the ceiling of a church,
And in the village of Sinassos there were many fine Greek
houses
With balconies and sunrooms falling slowly into ruin,

And three charming girls invited me into one of them.
In an upper-room, where no one lived, they showed me
  paintings
In which the painter had evoked the orthogonal boulevards
Of European cities he had never seen, and here a tale of exile
And expulsion lay concealed like a sharp pin in the folds of
  a blanket,
For, of the family who built the house, or their descendants,
  or neighbours,
Or the descendants of those neighbours, not one remained
  in Sinassos.
But nothing could dim the radiance of the girls, who posed
  for the camera
Before a hedge of roses, and all this while Andrew travelled
  with me,
And not once was there serious misunderstanding between
  us.
O distances and ghosts! Lakes that vanish, and smiling mouths
  of strangers!
O the descent of the sun in places where forgotten names
  are written,
It was well said:
  The road is lovely as if there were no death.

The Broken Steps

The sea like a river,
throat of the winds . . .
A green muscle
twists in the water . . .

A ship called *Jenghiz*,
a blue ship marked with rust
exchange tremendous greetings.

The wooden house hears them,
but turns away to terraced hills
concealing the carpenter's fruit trees.

*

The excavations never end —
driven through the streets, into
the very skulls of the inhabitants.

Exposed pipes rise
from ruinous sidewalks
like charmed snakes or swans' necks.

Dust in the eyes,
dust in the mouth, in the pages
of the book; streams of mud
on the Street of the Dice-Throwers,
down the long slope of White Rose Street.

*

Children's voices like glass-shards.
At nightfall the lights fail.

The affronted windows
of sunrooms darken,
and a church bell punctuates
the dialogues of pigeons.

*

The silks from Uzbekistan
are hung on the walls —
the red silk and the black,
embroidered with dull golds.

Against all reckoning
I am allowed this happiness.

Ai Khanum . . .

the banks of the Oxus,
Sogdiana's buried cities
cannot be so far off.
Only promontories
and rose bushes lie between.

On the Street of the Painted Kiosk
the awnings are unfurled.

Each evening everything is destroyed,
everything is reconstructed
in a spirit of ignorance and longing
and a child calls for his mother —

Anné! Anné! . . .

*

I am much closer now
to what I desired.

In a black casing
in the bank's museum
I saw King Menander's face —
his long nose, his high
cheek-bones, his lips —

the whole no larger than
a finger-nail,
but perfect as anything can be,
representing wisdom on a coin.

*

The judas trees are over.
Their fallen purples smudge the paths.

The season of green plums arrives,
and perslane returns
to the restaurant tables.

At the time of mating rams
a wind blows from the Pleiades.

Vines still festoon the streets,
hiding housefronts as a beard
might hide a face, but the wine-
cellars under the hill are empty.

Many miles to the south
nomads are folding their black tents,
eyeing the rifts in the mountains
but the steps are broken, vanish under
grass like the seats of a lost theatre.

Against all reckoning,
I have come this far.

It has begun again, the ascent
to summer's scorched plateau —

Anatolia, my sister
dead these two months.

2 Portraits

1. MIRABEAU BUONAPARTE LAMAR HIGGINS

Though hardly broiling by Baltimore standards
the heat is intense enough
that even Sibelius at his most blizzard-
blasted is beginning to warm up (the lakes
thawing out, the mosquitoes rising in clouds).

I don't take it lying down, mind you:
I massacred the flying ants at the door,
and went to the shopping mall to buy Ravel,
thinking that all that Gallic perfectionism
might do the trick, but it wilted in short order —

hardly more cooling than Elgar
the pavane swaddled in velvet . . .

Boys hurl themselves heedless into the Bosphorus,
and, in those circumstances, knowledge is a burden:
I've seen the black streams that feed it,
the armadas of plastic bottles drifting south
to decorate the Marmara. (Research project:

in what godforsaken repository
does all this stuff end up?)

O quays! O islands!
My table beneath the pines,
cool, marble halls of shopping malls,
municipal fountains, the tree
of swimming trunks in Iznik, vacant
waters of the lake, with what
passionate exactitude I dream of you all!

But that afternoon in the hollow
of the Baltimore sculpture garden
was the worst. Then, with no melody
for memorial I truly felt like
the deadest of dead Infantas.

2. MESSAGE (LEYLA TIRYAKIOĞLU)

Thank you for your kind invitation,
but when it started to rain
I was over on the neighbouring continent
feeling sick with a friend in her new apartment.

On the terrace there were many
green-upholstered chairs,
and having seated ourselves on two of them,
we began to look calmly about us
as if reading a score for three orchestras.

In one direction there were trees,
a swimming pool, domes and birdhouses.
We heard the excited yelling of a crowd
like a kind of wall thrown into the air.
In the other direction there were
fortresses and suspension bridges.
Minarets began to glow. Boats
Like bugs moved about on the water,

and a storm kept circling
above all of these things,
lashing at them, soaking them
randomly as if unable to decide

what to do next like a bored child.
There were patches of sulphur-yellow sky.
We laughed when the streets flooded.
The rubble of a tomb fled past us, foaming!

So this is how I was occupied
when you called and the machine
recited its stupid snatch of melody.

Flute Music

Beyond a long glass wall,
built to protect us from the spray,
the haze was deepening.
The Asian suburbs began to fade,
and the roar of their traffic —
distant but enveloping
when the wind was favourable —
was cut off, as if a huge, unwashed
window had been silently closed.
At a nearby table four Greek priests
were deep in a conversation
I longed to understand, and Selçuk
peered down into the ruins of his lunch,
and said: 'I think this bluefish
must have been a philosopher.
It has very thick bones.'

It was nearing winter.
Our footsteps clattered like cavalry
between the shuttered houses
of the rich and the exiled. A boy
rode by on a bike. The priests
turned a corner, and vanished.
I began to doubt that I had seen them.
They were, perhaps, visitors from
another time, which like them had vanished —
its towers broken. Only, the swing
of their long skirts, the black gleam
of their hair remained for a time
suspended in emptiness through which
yellow leaves as big as hands fell
unswerving to the cobbles. The air
stung my eyes, was a dense element

through which it seemed hard to move,
except at the pace of a procession.
And Selçuk said: 'On the boat we can breathe.'
The water was motionless, and on its surface
fishermen had drawn white circles,
which gulls in their hundreds attacked.
There was no horizon. The boat
moved like a spider across a wall.
We talked of music, the State Opera,
and his flute: 'It is very valuable,
the best make, very expensive.
My friends say I should sell it.
It would solve so many problems,
but I will not sell my flute.'

We were approaching an island,
the smallest of the group.
Dark creeper spilled down its red cliffs.
Pines and cypresses serrated its spine,
and in among them appeared
the red-tiled roof of a solitary house.
Who lived there? No boats came and went.
'Ah,' said Selçuk, 'that is a long story.
It begins, I think, in the fifteenth century.
At that time the sultan had a minister,
an Armenian of whom he was very fond,
and one day the sultan asked him:
"My friend what can I give you
that would fulfil your heart's desire?"
The Armenian thought for a moment,
and replied: "Sire, perhaps an island,
just a little island." And it was done,
and his descendants lived there
for many generations until the last
of them sold it to a rich old man
who had a young and beautiful wife —

so young and beautiful that there was
much talk among the islands,
in the boats passing back and forth.
They heard nothing. God had granted them
a daughter, and they were happy,
but it is said that if others watch
your life too closely it brings bad luck,
and suddenly this charming lady died
of a cancer, and the old man sold the island
for next to nothing and moved away,
dying himself a year or two later.
Their daughter was left all alone.
I don't know what happened to her,
but once, when she was very small,
we played games on the terrace of her father's house,
and her mother came through the shadows
of the pines, carrying a tray of cool drinks.'

The boat moved into open water,
but the way ahead remained hidden.
The city had been removed like a slide
from a projector. It was as though
we had embarked, unprepared, for an unknown
landfall, perhaps some northern outpost
of the forgotten Bosporan Kingdom.
We would travel there through fog and silence,
wrapped in the dense odour of tallow and furs,
encountering no monsters save absence . . .

Then a cold wind crossed the deck,
and very dimly lights began to appear
as if emerging from a great depth,
and the world began to move again,
but uneasily like a night-ferry
in crowded water, burdened.

Elegy, Replica, Echo
In Memoriam John Griggs 1941-1991

Your inanimate double, Ioannis,
was perhaps the little column of green onyx
that stood in a corner of the forum, or the statue
of some distinguished exarch weathered almost to nothing . . .
In your last days you had grown very thin.

The church I thought a poor thing —
dark, for they have covered the crossing
with a windowless dome, and between the nave
and the choir empty ages intervened. Yet you were there,

Ioannis, under the cloth of gold brocade
that the priest anointed, dipping a bundle of twigs
into a cup of holy water, and behind me two women —
good friends of yours — wept, unconsoled by music.

The words of the ancient hymn had been altered,
I noticed, in accordance with new conventions,
and the high notes of the chant cracked
as the priests took you away, surrounded by
tall candles, into the mouth of heaven.

As we entered the school a peacock cried out
in the garden, and I shivered. I saw it clearly,
setting atop the sundial, turning its turquoise neck,
but when I emerged, only moments later, it had gone,
and the gardener knew nothing of it.

Then a cat climbed up the steps, uttering loud cries
of greeting, and rubbed itself against my legs.
I remembered that in life you had been very fond of cats,
and I bent down to converse with the animal.

Bozuk Para

Something is wrong,
but something is also right, or
will at least *do for now*. Always so.
The cat, for example, is called 'Plume'
for obvious reasons, but it's her paws
I like best. Large and sturdy,
they seem to make the house stand up straight
even when the kitchen floor's under two inches
of water, and the newly-arrived guests
can be heard splashing about, making
the best of it, as we must I suppose,
like survivors of a mudslide.
Of course, she has her mad scenes, the house too —
its shutters thudding in the wind,
hanging off their hinges, the light fixtures
indulging in bad special effects,
as if all of this were a pantomime
of such unsurpassed tawdriness and boredom
that the child-audience dozed. And then,
the frenzied skittering of claws on wooden boards
is heard. Besides, I'd swear that roofbeam's
getting lower, and have the lumps to prove it.
I reel into the wall, dizzy . . .
The repeated blows are making me stupider
by the day, which is sort of relaxing,
like lying down in the middle of a landscape
without even a tree or a gas station,
just grass really, long grass I'd guess . . .

So this is exile, is it?
Can it be, if you wanted to leave
in the first place, at no emperor's behest?
In fact even the way the local transvestite

saunters down the street,
demurely dressed in a long green skirt,
seems familiar as a storefront in Liverpool,
although, like everything else in these parts,
more extreme in its manner of expression:
ugly-beautiful, beautiful-ugly, and so on.

And what about those letters home —
scores of them — that I should be writing,
full of wit, advice and melancholy?
I've tried, but all I came up with was:

'Hi! I really like it here. The people are nice,
and you don't have to pretend to be happy all the time,
which is a big relief I can tell you. You can sit
in a café looking just as glum as you please,
and no one will think anything of it. If a tear escapes,
and embarks on the long journey to your shirt collar,
well, that's fine too. Anyone who looks in your direction
will just say to themselves, "Ah, life is like that sometimes",
then continue drinking their coffee,
while gazing out sympathetically towards the water,
which is just beginning to shimmer a little
after several days of unseasonal rainstorms,
and the smoke from his cigarette makes a nimbus.'

Language Poem: 2000 BC — 2000 AD

Everything begins like this:
all ideas radiate from a centre, don't they?
like the spokes of a chariot wheel?

In the steppes to the east of the Urals
they knew something, and knew it early.
In their new-fangled vehicles
they fanned out to east and west and south —

south, where the easy pickings were,
those cities with their lumbering ox-carts,
and irrigation systems. So
the dull civilization of the Indus valley
was destroyed, and the words I write
began to form like fungus growths,
their spores carried on the spokes
of chariot wheels.

Everyone wanted the new device,
but it didn't come cheaply.
First you had to build the thing,
then there were the horses,
the drivers, the shield-bearers,
the grooms, the veterinarians,
and the provisions for all of these,
not to mention a swarm of clerks
and quartermasters, without whom
the entire enterprise would collapse.

Kings competed:
to lack a sufficient number
of chariots was to be no one,
was to be smashed like a picket fence

in the path of stampede. Thus,
at Kadesh, Kings Ramses II
and Muwatallis II mustered
over three thousand chariots each
at a total cost of four million shekels,
but the battle was indecisive,
and the armies turned homewards
accompanied by an enormous
rumbling of wheels,
and very soon the introduction
of cavalry rendered the chariot almost
as useless for military purposes
as a bicycle. It did not vanish,
but assumed a happier character,
essential to the amusements of great cities,
featured in sporting events, pageants
and parades with garlands and phalluses,
or else it was 'translated to the skies',
god-driven, rolling over clouds, towing the sun.

Even when these beliefs were dead,
it still aroused strong passions.
In Byzantium
fans of the rival chariot teams
wore their hair long
'in the Hunnish fashion',
and wore the colours of their teams —
the Greens and the Blues —
and persons of the wrong colour,
discovered in the wrong place,
were killed out of hand.

Perhaps, as chariots rattled by,
splendid and archaic,
violent memories were stirred,
but the ensuing riots were

displeasing to the government,
and, in time, the event was restricted,
becoming a mere ritual —

Lacquered relic, memory of a memory,
knuckle-bone lost
in the sub-basement
of an otherwise erased palace
of formerly vast extent.

And the stadium fell into ruin.
This was in the thirteenth century;
yet the language of the chariot remains;
it rumbles in our throats;
it rolls across our tongues,

freshly this morning, here and in Rome,
as the snow falls or the rain.

Imbrogion

Exhausted from the journey
through the rains of the plateau
I drank wine and fell asleep at once.

Later, much later, and still asleep
I walked out onto the balcony,
bowing my head beneath the low eaves,

and woke there, and found myself
looking out, amazed, at ruined towers
and white façades of mansions

unpeopled for a thousand years,
where the crowded houses of my neighbours
should have been. For long moments

everything remained as it was not;
no mists marred the lines of masonry,
sharp as an architect's elevation;

no fretful children wailed, or late car stalled.
I stumbled back as if thrown into the room,
but what had been the bed was now

a mound of red earth littered with rubble —
a looted grave, a horror. My hand, not I,
moved to the switch, and so I was saved,

but from what? Madness or vision?
I sat for a time, a book unopened in my hand,
and remembered Isaura's lost towers.

I thought of Illos ascending the spiral stair
of his palace as he plotted against his friend
the infamous Emperor Zeno

(who, it is said, was interred alive)
and I grew calm in the knowledge
of what I had seen, of what haunted me.

The Names of Kings

In a poem of nineteen twenty,
Phanar's and Alexandria's most renowned son
writes of Indian coins inscribed with names of kings,
barbarous names, impossible to pronounce —
Eboukratintaza, Eramaiaza and so on,
then on the reverse he finds that the names
appear in pure, hellenic form as
Hermaios, Eukratides, Straton, Menander
and his heart is touched: 'How the Greek stops
at once, how he is moved as he reads . . .'

We who are not Greek,
since we must read this poem in translation,
may be puzzled by the profound sadness
of these words (which we understand
at once without understanding),
and we resort to the notes provided
by the translator for those who may not
be versed in the history of the Greek East.

From them we learn that Eukratides
'was one of the most powerful of the Bactrian kings',
and that he 'made great conquests in Northern India',
and Hermaios, it is also allowed, was a king
(though nothing more is said of him), but Straton,

Straton, we discover to our amazement,
was no more than a peripatetic philosopher
at the court of Ptolemy Philadelphus.
As to Menander, the most beautiful of the names,
and the one that ends the poem, it is
misascribed to 'an Athenian comic poet'.

How absurd, how regrettable this is!
Has it ever been known for poets
or philosophers to mint coinage?
Who would accept such a currency?
And has it not been clearly stated
that these are the names of kings?

Thus Straton was a king in his own right,
not a dependent of the depraved Lagidae
and it was Menander, King and Saviour,
who ruled the Greek dominions in India
when their prosperity was at its height
who led a great army with companies of Cretan
archers along the valley of the Ganges
to burn the city of Pataliputra;
Menander who was so loved for his wisdom
that he was thought to have ended his days
in the saffron robes of a Buddhist monk.
According to another tradition, however,
he died like a true Hellene, vainly defending
Bactria against the barbarians.

If it were otherwise,
if he were merely a comic poet
(famous to be sure, but one whose works
survive only in fragments of
a dispiriting, mechanical dullness)
then words that should have taken us
beyond Zagros and the Indus,
to the far reaches of that diaspora
in which the Greeks vanished like windblown dust,
leaving only coins as monuments,
are reduced to pedantry and farce. Yet
all of this has been accomplished
with the best intentions and great labour,
and how keenly the son of Phanar and Alexandria

would have appreciated the bitter irony of the error —
he who had celebrated so many defeats
himself defeated and betrayed, not by an enemy,
but a friend, a devout scholar, almost a lover . . .

Under Mount Anamas

1. It is an efficient method,
and many centuries old —

two poles, two whittled branches
or stems of poplar, one vertical,

the other diagonal, balancing:
dip it and up the water comes,

cold, clear. Under Mount Anamas
waters are many and have been worshipped.

Great stones were set beside pools
and carved with figures of women

praising the sky (weathered now,
their faces like used soap).

On other occasions nothing was done —
the water unadorned, persistent.

Years meant nothing to it
as it fed the colours of the lake.

Carp gulped it. Women came
from the palace, washed their faces.

2. In the untidy, municipal garden
was a fragment of marble vine-scroll,

and a tombstone showing a woman
with arms folded beneath compact breasts.

The boys were frightened of the dog
whose jaws snapped shut inches from my hand.

Uncertain where we were being taken,
I was reluctant to get into the boat.

The blue corpse of a dragonfly lay
motionless on the water surface.

On the island, under the wheeling gulls,
in the collapsed tower I picked up

a bright segment of turquoise tile
that had outlasted seven hundred years,

but lost it only days later
in some crevice of a hotel room.

3. He had chosen the site well —
a spring, a screen of willows,

a natural terrace overlooking
the lake's vast mirror,

but before his palace could be
completed, the prince was poisoned,

and it was the murderer who sat in
Kubadabad's cool halls,

when summer burned the plains —
the murderer, his own son . . .

4. When the car stopped, a sharp odour
of dried dung greeted us.

The dust was thick, but the people
had the manners of courtiers.

Under its new coat of plaster and paint
the mosque resembled a bungalow:

only the carved doorframe
and the blunt minaret showed

any trace of age or distinction,
but when the old men admitted us

my mouth fell open at the sight
of that grove of artificial trees

blossoming into honeycombs,
stalactites and pendant seed-pods

at dark blue flowers and black tendrils
uncurling on vermilion roofbeams.

5. Robbed stone, ashlar.
Stacked reeds and sherds.

Cattle skirting the edge of the marsh,
whisking their tails against flies.

Not much for the visitor to see —
intimate rooms lying open to the sky,

the absent images
glazed, star-shaped,

detached from the rubble vault
the owl hooting in Afrasiah's halls . . .

But still the prince raises his wine cup,
the women smile and the donkey brays.

Aunt Petka's Earrings

I presented the earrings
to Aunt Petka
in the suburb of Bebek.
The maid was slatternly
and the key to the cabinet lost.

Yachts had replaced
the fishing boats, but because
of the hip injury
we could not cross into
the gardens of Asia.

Aunt Petka wore a peignoir,
for which she apologized.
We looked at photographs
of her handsome nephew, her dead
husband in a dapper suit,
posed with her in London or Venice.
She said: 'When will he come?
the spring, the summer?
We must go to the islands soon.'

She too had once stayed at
the *Grand Hôtel de Londres*.
I loved the lamps like lilies,
the ridiculous number of mirrors
and defunct radios,
but tipped the wrong youth twice.

The evenings were written
in long lines of Persian.
Gusts of laughter blew in
from a nearby café. There was

also the sound of church bells
in the afternoon, muffled but close,
and, more distantly, muezzins . . .

At sunset a choking stench
crawled over the balcony rail
and sat in the room until dawn.

The waiter was suspect.
My friend wore a hat with a frayed brim.
We photographed the bellhops.

Sometimes it seemed that I had entered
the precincts of a childhood
that was not my own, or not entirely.

On my way to the flower market
I stopped at a brown archway
that led into a courtyard where
a vine stretched its thin limbs out
towards the windows of abandoned buildings.

I saw a line of four, green doorways,
each marked with a brass cross.
The church beyond them was dim,
as if underwater.
There were paintings
that imitated mosaics
of the fourteenth century,
and a bouquet of flowers
only a few days old, lying before
an icon of the Virgin,

and it was as though I heard a voice —
an old voice, dry and hooded,
the voice of a woman who said:

'Take blessings to my grandsons.
Tell them I am still here.
They live in America,
and they are handsome as statues,
statues made of glass.
I have not seen them, but sometimes
the light falls through them
and covers my face, so I appear
a young girl again.'

Of course, this was only smoke and whispers,
and, in the end, we sailed to the islands,
and inhaled the scent of the pines.

How we longed to stay beneath
the tiled cupolas of the *Hotel Splendid!*
How the horse-drawn carriages jolted us!
On the path to the monastery
we tied votive rags to the bushes,
as many hundreds of people had done before us.
We drank wine as we looked down
on the burnished breastplate of the sea.

We were astonished to see
so much bougainvillea in bloom
so early in the year, but Petka —
Aunt Petka — did not come with us.

In Khorkum

the wounded bird sang in the tree
and the kings were remembered
when the mother wept and the father went away
leaving the red slippers for his son
who had stopped speaking

and the martyrs were remembered
and the ancestors
who rode into battle on purple horses

and the bird still sang in the summit of the poplar
as water flowed in the canals
and a salt breeze blew in from the lake
where boats sailed towards the island of the almonds

and the pruning implements writhed
on the blue wall of the house
longing to escape into the orchards

then the trees whispered prophesies
as they had done in Alexander of Macedon's day
and ravens' eggs were painted with the colours of the fields
where the earth crumbled under the horses' hooves

and the father sat in mid-ocean sailing to America

and the prince rode into the heart of the rock
(the Raven's Rock the Rock of Van)
and the prince said *I will not come out*
until the world is less wicked
until wheat grains grow big as rosebuds

the world stayed wicked and the rock stayed shut
yet clouds like winged heads still rose above the mountains
and boats sailed by where now there are none
and the boy found a voice in the wood
he had whittled for his father who was gone

then the scent of apricots covered the fields
and clear water ran beside the streets of Van
below the rock where the prince had vanished

then the uncle's corpse was thrown against the door of the *vank*
and the grandmother stepped in the blood
then god was dead for her and the church burned

but the plough still sang in the fields
and the sun danced like a dervish in the trees

and one year later the son was born
and soon the father departed leaving the red slippers
and boats sailed towards the island of the almonds
where once King Gagik's palace had stood
and candles burned before the tombs of ancestors
in the place where the madmen were chained

and the prince said *I will not come out*
until the world is less wicked
until barley grains are large as walnuts
and the earth could not bear the weight of his horse

then a regiment of butchers
descended on the villages
in the valley of the Hayk

then the fire rained down from the rock
(the Raven's Rock the Rock of Van)
then the fire ran through the fields

then the fire erased the images of the martyrs
that painted books in the halls of Varak

a woman appeared naked at the gates of the city

and the demon sat installed above the flames
dressed in an elegant suit manicured
amusing himself with a French novel

and the people of Shadakh were killed
and the people of Berghri the people of Harput

then the mother buried everything she possessed
in the garden of Aikezdan
in hopes of a resurrection
and walked long days with her son
over the hard ground
eating wild herbs unripe fruit
passing by Massis crossing river Arax

and four years later the mother died
still longing for the home of her ancestors
died by a leaking window in midwinter

in the arms of her son who travelled on
to Tiflis to Batum and Bolis
sailing to America to the father he did not love
and the scent of the apricots followed him
the taste of the salt and cries of birds above the rock

then in poverty and long weeks of rain
his mother's embroidered apron began to unfold
and wheat grains grew big as rosebuds
barley grains were as large as walnuts

and twenty years passed in fulfilment
then the paintings burned and the dead mother spoke

my son what can I do
colour and contour have gone from my face
scorpions nest in my heart
child you have wandered enough

The Tour

It was an achievement of a kind —
to have found a driver who did not know the way
from the university to the old city . . .

I swore in frustration as we diverged
into districts of dust and breeze blocks,
unfinished, half-ruined. Washing fluttered
from fifth storeys without an outer wall.
Songbirds sang in their cages beside plants
sprouting from oil cans. Roosters strutted before
pharmacies and auto-repair shops,
while a ram was pulled from a Mercedes
and dragged towards the butcher's still kicking.

We were lost in a dull swarm of cabs and buses,
amid dwellings migrants from emptiness
had built overnight, but the students only smiled,
glad of this break from the grey necessities of grammar.

Then, as if a fog had suddenly rolled aside,
we emerged in the region of the Edirne Gate
and saw the banded towers, the parapets, the rift
where the marble king had died. In the moat gypsies
had draped bushes with the bright rags of their laundry.

The way into the city was narrow, the stones pitted.
We plunged into a tangle of crowded lanes,
disorderly but welcoming. I was running on instinct.
I said: 'Go straight ahead. No, turn left,
up that steep street. Something about it looks
familiar. I feel it like a phantom limb . . .'

And, before long we arrived at the doorway of a hospital,
built for Roxelana, beloved wife of Süleyman,
whom the Turks call 'Law-Giver', and we 'Magnificent',
though he had his most gifted son strangled by mutes,
in part to please his wife. But how much we admired
the octagonal courtyard, the chimneys of the soup kitchen —
each one a small pavilion. The gardens were unkempt
but lovely (the trees thin and graceful).
The road wound about like a river, bringing us
to the shrine of a saint whose name was Hyacinth.

We saw the tombs, the mosque that concealed a church,
and the ruined tree, leaning on its concrete crutch
like a beggar. It was December, but not yet cold.
Only the Armenian priest was unkind, refusing us
admission to the bleak, grey church of Surp Kevork,
but the students were not discountenanced. When the doors
were shut in their faces they examined with delight
the burnished reliefs, touching them, stroking them.
The gates of Eden were also closed, guarded by militant angels.

In a square shaped like a crushed star,
stalls were heaped with fish, as they had been
day after day, in that same place, since the time
of the first Constantine. Beneath the belfry
of Saint Menas we entered a carpenters' workshop
that was also the tomb of Saints Karpos and Papylos.
It was in the form of a domed rotunda.
It was built entirely of brick. The students
were astonished that anything so old and so fine
could be used in this way. Light entered through
an aperture at the centre of the dome,
dimly illuminating the carpenters' tools.

The old street of triumphs and processionals
had wandered a little from its straight path

47

as if extreme old age had made it forgetful.
but still it led us to the roofless basilica
of Studion. From the locked gate
we admired the columns of verd antique
the labyrinthine patterns of the floor
and came at last to the Golden Gate —
place of entrance, place of statues,
gilded statues of Emperors, Victory and Fate
(its arches walled up now, the statues gone),
and I thought of the entrance of Heraclius
in the year six hundred and twenty eight.
He came with plunder and elephants,
having confounded the Persians. The way
was strewn with flowers; silks and carpets
were draped from the windows and the balconies,
but in a short space, the merest flicker of a leaf,

he would suffer loss beyond imagining —
Syria and Egypt lost, and with them
Antioch and Alexandria, those great cities . . .

and once more he returned to his capital,
this time in terror, his mind half-unhinged,
and the people were convinced that all of this
was punishment for his sinful union
with his niece Martina, whom they detested,
and he who had been magnanimous and brave
grew morbidly cruel, dying miserably
from an infection of the urinary tract.

On either side of the gate rose square towers
faced with white marble, one pierced by
a narrow door, too low to enter without stooping.
Beyond it, ramps and stairs twisted upwards
through the mass of stone. At the halfway point
the lights failed: it was completely dark.

We lit improvised tapers, emerging at length
on the broad summit of the tower.

Pale sunlight poured down on the Marmara,
and its stalled armada of tankers, container-ships,
on the long, northward arc of the city walls,
on open fields once marred by reeking tanneries.

The students posed for a group portrait against
a backdrop of machicolations and the sea,
but the elevation made me giddy and my knees weak,
so I descended alone, stumbling in the dark.

This seemed to go on for a long time,
as if I were descending into the earth,
perhaps to that crypt or martyrium
where, legend has it, the Last Emperor,
the eleventh Constantine, lies at rest,
either asleep, or turned to stone,
but I heard nothing, saw nothing.
The stone did not become flesh,

and if I had encountered him
what would he have said? He was
hard-pressed, had no time to record
his thoughts or marry, no time
at the end of a thousand years.
Stumbling in darkness. Alone.

At the base of the tower was a room
that had once been a prison, nearly windowless,
and filled with a skeletal structure
of struts and brackets, whose unhappy purpose
we could only guess at. Near its centre
was a well into which we dropped stones
and coins to test the depth. No sound came.

If there were ghosts here they were voiceless,
but the fear the place had once inspired
was real and irreducible as granite.

Yet we had escaped it all, were free
to return to our homes along a road
that led past mosques and fountains,
and the students were once again quiet,
tired perhaps, holding their notebooks,
as the light died on the windows of Asia.

Desert Song

And so, as in the opening of a *quasida*
I address the remains of a campfire, —

the one we shared in the waterless outer precincts
of the riot-torn city . . . Beloved! O
moon among flickering lanterns, I am on my way, —

my light skiff negotiates with ease
the rusting hulks and gun-boats of the port,

and soon I am well advanced along the Grand Canal,
passing the Green Mosque
skirting the Tower Of The Winds until

I disembark at the Square Of The Souks, —
famed in history and travelogue . . .

And here is something to mock the visitor,
for at the centre of the square lies
a massive compass-star drawn in white mosaic
on a ground of dull, red stone, —

and a compass is what you will need
(and of course you didn't think to bring one)
for it is easy to lose your way in this place

amidst the din
of metal workers and public address systems,
amidst the scent of grilling meats and burning charcoal,

among the roses and grottoes of the Monteverdi Gardens,
in the sound of rebecs, ouds, tramcars, telephones,
cavalry, and shells exploding along the besieged corniche!

Here are numberless distractions and alarms:
sometimes a man swaying under the weight of a fluttering
    totem
of lottery tickets will fall at your feet, smiling

as if in death, or a woman with a scar across her throat
will call out confused words from the dim patch of an alley
(and she, you at once recognize, is a visitant
from another poem, not this one you are living)

— indeed, in no other city is panic so likely
to attack the stranger, and yet considerations
of religious taboo and military strategy
forbid the publication of maps. But courage,

oh my star! for I am still on my way,
clutching grimly at my water-flask, eyes fixed
on the exposed mechanism of the casino's clock tower,

which is like our hearts, like the rich and complex feelings
that should be coming into play at this moment, amidst
the striking of bells and the ululations of muezzins,

if only I could find you. But, as is inevitable,
the sky begins to darken as if an immense shutter were
    sliding into place,
a fog rises from the canals and a swarm of starving people
stumbles through the narrow streets.

I am thrown aside into the crumbling pavilion
of a disused public fountain, and fear,
like a line of ants begins to crawl up my spine.

Malicious birds, carriers of disease, have devoured the
    crumbs I left as a trail,
and examination of my pockets reveals that I carry
no note of your address. The crowd thickens

and begins to chant in unison words
my phrase book does not record; they begin to lacerate their
    faces
with their nails; they begin to strike out at one another
confusedly with branches.
I dare not emerge from my hiding place,
and I am still on my way. Forever now.

Gabrielle's Balcony

1. The road began to descend
between punctured buildings —
but towards what? With

the ghost of a laugh, the driver
announced: 'The city centre!'
and threw his hand out
towards darkness, leaving it,
for a moment, printed there
as on the wall of a cave.

I could see nothing. Not
one light shone.

*

2. In an old quarter, close
to an abandoned synagogue
with yellow walls,
I stepped in blood, then
washed my shoes in water
that spilled from a broken main

down into
courtyards where women
perilously ascended
exposed staircases, riven
with cracks, turning to dust . . .

They had the kind of faith
that once was given only to saints.

*

3. In the camps
sheep were marked for slaughter.
So many of them, amid
stinking mounds, and the buzz
of commerce. Ahead of us
the procession of expensive cars
halted, as if a moment
of silence had been observed.
The driver said 'I hate no one',
meaning that there were many
who were worthy of hatred.
The ruins of the stadium
were suspended above us,
but strangely the ferris-wheel
on the corniche kept turning.

*

4. To return is dangerous.
I had returned, and where
the Square of Stars had been
found only mounds, pits,

stumps of columns —
the destroyed city
beneath the destroyed city.

Clouds rolled over the mountains,
and approached the eastern suburbs.

*

5. The sanctuary stood
above a small, clear stream.
Nothing had touched it.

Below the statues
poppies starred the grass.

A lake of mist filled the valley
(a wedding veil, a shroud)
and beyond it, to the south,
were the snows of a great mountain.
I had seen nothing more lovely,

but I had read the map
of the territories —
torn and stained, apportioned
to warring powers and peoples.

*

6. Drifts of trash
blew across the vineyards,
and a handsome boy in a red shirt
rode a chestnut mare
through the ruins of a palace.

In vast basements beneath
the Shrine of the Dead Father
the geometric floor-mosaics

were preserved. At the gate
a soldier pointed his gun
towards me, then approached to ask
if I would take his photograph.

*

7. Gabrielle showed me her beautiful home.
She was very elegant, and wore a brooch
in the shape of an artist's palette.

We walked out onto the balcony.
We admired the garden, the pillars
and the high ceilings, then she paused,
and said, with no special emphasis:

'My sister was sitting right here
when the shell came through the ceiling.
It made a very small hole, then it exploded.'

Later we dined in a restaurant
decorated with murals
of a vaguely Pompeian cast.

Beautiful walls, beautiful ceilings —
rise into the air of the Middle Sea,
remain visible at a great distance!

*

8. On the summit
Of an isolated hill
I came upon a temple
built by a king in
homage to an emperor.

In the village below,
young men (exhumed,
unwounded from their graves)
paraded in pink and turquoise suits.

It was a fine evening to be out walking.

A Book of Complaints

In Istanbul
it is impossible to buy
good umbrellas,

and all the roofs
of all the houses leak,

yet the rains are heavy
and prolonged, so today —

a day of rain —
it is with a certain
weariness that I look out

at denuded plane-trees
and smoke rising from
the precinct-house chimney,

while at my back I hear,
persistently, the kitchen's
dismal water music.

In the evenings
my principal diversion
is the interpretation of mould-stains.

*

In Istanbul
the frequent power outages
make romantics of us all.

Reverting to pen and paper,
to simple printed pages
bathed in the glow of candles,

as the machines die
we begin to feel distinctly
Ottoman, even Byzantine —

Prince Cem, Anna Comnena,
or old Procopius
composing his slanders by night,
cursing the Sleepless One.

*

In Istanbul
the number of potholes
might be considered

a perverse compensation
for the relative lack
of sidewalks. Each week

new trenches appear on the streets
(it is one of the haunting
mysteries of the place)

and small crowds gather
to peer down into them
quizzically and a little sadly

as if they could read the future
in mud as rich as coffee-grounds,
and a tangle of electric cables

*

As your taxi crawls
along the coast
towards the palaces

and some affluent fool
in a Range Rover
entirely blocks your way,

you look out with a sharp,
hypertrophied longing
to the great waterway

that glitters nearby
abjured, unused. Please
let us not mention Tantalus.

*

Istanbul —
I have discovered
the root of all your problems.

It is because your middle-classes
live in apartments
overlooking the Bosphorus —

apartments designed
by lunatic children!

Mektup

If you receive this letter,
if you open it (if it is opened for you
by some smiling attendant) if you then
remember to read it, and put it down
on the bedside table next to the photograph
of your eldest child and her sons,
you will immediately forget that it is there,
forget every word of it, forget that it ever came,
and this freedom to say *anything* leaves me
tongue-tied like the child you remember,
having nothing particular to confess,
no cure or revelation, only: Dear M. I moved

to escape the children and the dogs,
and the nice but strange woman
who stole my doormat; so now I live
in a building called 'Clover Palace'
(and coloured accordingly)
on the Street of the Water Carrier's Garden
(although there are no gardens to speak of)
and I have covered the floors with rugs from the Caucasus
with rugs woven by Kurdish women in the mountains
of Hakkari, and I have purchased two vases
of a beautiful, opaque glass, one blue, one green.
Each morning I sit at my desk and drink tea
without milk in the Turkish fashion, and also,
as you will have guessed, smoke too many cigarettes
as I look out over red rooftops towards the Bosphorus,
which, in winter, is a veritable Book of Preludes,
the pages turning from blue to brilliant silver, to white
when a fog descends and half the world vanishes.

Then it is hard for me to remember where I am,
what city or landmass. The fog is bitter
and fills my mouth, and often a ship passes —
a ship as long as a city block — and seems to
summon me, who cannot follow. Hours pass
imagining its destination. And this is not a dream,
though it has the colours and the architecture, the sense,
also, of being at the centre of an enormous cloud.

I would like to tell you that I am happy,
but that is too simple and tempts fate. (I am
happiest when I forget the ghost you have become.)
Here, my sadness finds a home in the thick smoke
of coffee houses, and the tombs of the southern shore,
the orange groves in the dead cities . . .

Who were these people, citizens
of another time, who were so close to their dead
that they buried them in the market place
in tombs adorned with winged psychopompic figures?
The inscriptions can be deciphered only in fragments.
I came to a wall, and thorns tore my hands.
At Sura I stumbled and fell on my way down
the steep slope to the temple of Apollo Surius.
At Andriake, at Balbura, at Karkabo . . .
But I don't know why these places mean so much
to me, or what I am seeking in the ruins.
Repose of a kind, compiling a Dictionary of Lost Things . . .

To you, of course, these must seem dry concerns,
since you live in a place where everything
is continually vanishing, where memory is ruined
as surely as any arch or dome, but I
cannot forget the day I found you at the end
of a long corridor garishly lit by the cheapest
chandeliers, washed by urinous piped music.

You were lying on your side, face averted,
saying, 'What's that *mess* over there in the corner?'
as you pointed towards hyacinths, and a vase
of carnations, blood-red and beginning to decline.

One idea remained to you
like an old coin you had rubbed smooth,
and that was *to go home* when no such place existed —
lost beyond hope of restoration,
the spoils stolen, the tesserae that once composed
the intricate picture of our lives together
and apart, stripped from the wall, and the wall
reduced to rubble, reclining figures
of husband and wife beheaded. Mother,

it is January in Istanbul,
and the weather is bad, almost as bad
as it is in Manchester, and I want to send you greetings,
but I will not insult your misery
by wishing your New Year happy, as it cannot be.
I send you all the love that makes no difference at all.

Forgotten Orchestras

1. Night stands to the left,
  divided from us.
  The serving-girl approaches
  the dead man,
  who reclines on the couch,
  bearded, robust as in life.
  His wife sits, veiled,
  on the side of day. The dead man
  looks at neither one, but stares
  down towards a sea losing its lustre,

  and that far point where
  lights will appear in
  the little harbour of Meis.

2. The river loses itself
  in the white reeds of the marsh,
  and a boy's voice rings out
  from the wood of the thornbush.

  Trust neither maps nor books,
  but grope your way over the rocks
  towards the stinking pool
  where jewelled fish once proposed
  ambiguous prophecies.

3. Submerged lintel, calm sea.
  The boat rides above the city,
  appearing to people gathered
  in the drowned market place
  as the conveyance of a god,
  but one who answers no prayers —

'Lord, raise our bones to the level
of a dry breeze in the summer grass.'

4.   On this shore the harbours shift —
a mile, two miles or ten —
inland, forgetting their purpose.

Sand fills them or silt,
sealed gulfs lose their salt,
yet the quays remain
and granaries mumble
the names of emperors.

5.   What are these figures
in the shadow of the rock?
Those on the right are not dancers,
as a sightless author tells,
for their hands are bound behind them,
and they seem to stagger all together,
in terror of falling. A stern male figure
rides stiffly before them, yet towards him
run a boy and a girl, their hands clasped.
Her skirts are flying out behind her
It is impossible to mistake their joy.

Perhaps it is all very simple.
Father, dear father, has come home
from the wars unharmed
with a fine haul of slaves in his train,
and his children understand at once
how much easier their lives will be.

6.   The theatre pulls a skirt of sand
over its forgotten orchestra

The stones, the stone women
are carried into exile:

Walled in, two thousand miles
from the light of their birth,
they no longer know themselves.

But the light remembers
like a mother, as it falls
through their vanished outlines.

The Black Gondola

I think of nothing.
Nothing comes to me —
a woman consisting
only of her veils,
colourless as water,

she neither stands nor sits,
but follows me
several paces back,

in the street,
beside the strait.
If I turn she vanishes.
She will not speak,

but I have spoken to her
often, too often,
for I must thank her.
She is rest and emptiness —

a bed without the bother
of a sheet or mattress,
a vacant pillow. And I say:

'Nothing,

how you have helped me!
In my confusion
it is to you I turn —
you always beside me
like a glass or a telephone,

and on certain evenings
when the world narrows
to a dark canal,
it is only your voice I hear,
and through you I become
capable of speech. O my

poverty, my shack —
widow, shadow, cloud!'

To the City

Part I

My Poetry

Because they didn't get it, and wanted to be polite,
critics used to call my poetry 'experimental'.
This always puzzled me. Was I some kind of scientist?
Was I planning to clone Mallarmé or an ox?
What did they mean? Uh. I always thought
it was just my heart talking about the things
I loved and hated, hated and loved, like Scriabin,

who was a very strange person,
or Gesualdo, who killed someone on a swing
and got away with it. In truth, I care little
about either of these composers. Ah, sadness and freedom!

How To Use This Book

It would be best to read it sitting down,
but it doesn't matter much where you are.
You could be sitting at your desk, or on a rock
by a fast-flowing stream, or even on the steps of a temple,
or in the dignified plaza of a major centre of finance.
You could also read it standing up, but *do not*,
on any account, read it while walking around:
you might fall into a hole or walk into a tree.
Reading the book in moving vehicles is permitted,
providing you are not the one doing the driving.
And really the whole purpose of the book
is to get you moving, to persuade you
to leave your comfortable room, urged on
by great gusts of enthusiasm and expectancy,
and to climb to the top of mountains
or to descend into abyssal valleys, and think
thoughts that wouldn't normally occur to you,
even if they are only on the lines of: 'Help!
I am miles from anywhere, menaced by a rabid dog,
and how will I get back to my hotel by nightfall?'
Although it disavows masochistic rigour,
the book thinks this might not be all bad. It is
opposed to all forms of complacency and routine,
and stale preconceptions are anathema to it.
It dislikes strict metre, and the idea that
the poet is inevitably agonized. Of course,
it is possible that in some places you will have
horrible experiences, but in others you are equally
sure to find radiance and mystery, unless you happen
to be the kind of dunderhead who wants
everything 'abroad' to be a repetition, as if travel
consisted merely of walking out of one living-room
into another, and then another and another.

What a fucking nightmare! The book abhors this,
and would probably advise you to live in a bunker
if that is your attitude, but if the book is in your hand,
if you are reading it while sitting or standing
or relaxing in a moving vehicle,
then you cannot be such a fatuous person.
You have already decided that you want to be
ASTONISHED, DAZZLED and CONFUSED.
You are already, in some sense, an avant-garde poet,
and the book will go with you all the way,
saying in Miltonic tones: 'Behold!', and again:
'Be bold! This destination with a name you can't pronounce
may turn out to be an iniquitous dump, but that
won't kill you will it? And it may be wonderful,
and you may fall in love with the light on a stone at evening.'
And so on. As you are using the book you may sometimes feel
that the book is using you. This is normal.
You must sometimes feel this way about your friends,
and, rest assured, the book is your friend.
It will give you accurate directions, but thinks
it might sometimes be useful if you got lost
like a child in a dark forest. In this way,

you will invite kindness and sympathy,
and suddenly a new path will emerge like a hoopoe
from a ruined tower, and you will encounter joy
in the form of a young woman gathering herbs. Or . . .
But who knows what you will encounter? Whatever it is,
the book urges you, with all its heart, to welcome it.
There are yellow and brown signs along the way,
except where there are none.

A Rhyme for Koray

Now we know these things —

Above the olive groves of Iznik
The figures on a sarcophagus
Float calmly through the sky
To which a ladder climbs aslant

But in Lydia the sky becomes
A vast blue Ionic scroll above
A lake that cannot mirror it —
It is a superimposition an invention

In Phrygia
Domain of the Mother
A lioness bites down towards
The pinnacles of rock
                    Elsewhere
Horses graze on clouds and a church
Hangs above a palace façade
In place of clouds that are not there

Or a half-dome shelters
A tomb a boat a bank of reeds
Now we know these things

The only rhyme for Koray is sky
And the beautiful door opens the book

A Short Divan

BARGYLIA

Colours poured down on the flags.
Wild iris crowded into a marble doorframe.
The small watersnake moved steadily upstream
accompanied by sharp cries of appreciation
for the effort it was making, the river was so strong
in contradiction. Was I travelling,
or had I arrived at the place I had always
wanted to be without (however) knowing it,
having been dragged here by some force
inexorable as money? The question was open:
before it might be asked I thanked everything
for its contribution and sympathy. Coffee was served.

The only solution — assuming one is needed —
is to plunge into the water or the ruins, to touch,
in either case, the bruised bloom of another world.
Nothing will be as you expected it to be, yet it is home
of a kind, with complex signatures you recognize.

ALARM

The kind man at the hotel said:
'Last night we thought you were going to burn the town down.'
Now Leyla is calm, but the gold flame of her hair is not.

INTERVAL

First comes the container ship *Alligator Pond*,
then comes the tanker *Adonis*,
and, darting between them, with a palpable air
of impudence, is a small fishing boat

named *Ali Reis*. Recaulked
and repainted, it will outlast them.

TALKING TO THE DEAD

I didn't think much of Aphrodisias,
but liked the restaurant I found nearby.
The parking-lot was crowded with tour buses,
so we asked the waiter if the service would be slow.
He spread his hands, and exclaimed: 'If you like!'
The olive oil was delicious, but at Aphrodisias —

Why did they move all the people away,
and destroy their beautiful village?

I have nothing against the dead,
but have always found interaction
with the living more rewarding,
however admirable the statues might be.

AYA SOFIA

And my brother said to me on first entering it,
'How does it stay up?'
This was a simple but intelligent question.

78

REVERSE ALCHEMY

The conference by the polluted gulf
was boring, even though its subject was not.
This is a talent academics have.

An oar rots on the filthy beach.

THE GLOOM OF TURKISH MUSIC

Sometimes the gloom of Turkish music
comforts me. I mean no one can be that unhappy
all the time can they? I thought when my mother died
I would be inconsolable, that it would be 'the end of me',
but it was not. She had declined and suffered,
and, to an extent, I had suffered with her, but now
she was no longer suffering, and I was not dead.
It felt strange, but sad and regrettable only in the sense
that everything is sad and regrettable, or potentially so.

I couldn't wait for the funeral to be over.
It was cold. She wasn't there.

VIOLETS

By the road to Karkabo
there were bright mauve flowers amid the rocks.
Sezer insisted they were violets. I said:
'No, these are cyclamen', but it was useless.
She was adamant. Eventually I said:
'OK. We will call them The Sezer Violets.'
Later we checked, and they were cyclamen.

MALLARMÉ

I am sick of hearing that
'The only true subject of poetry is poetry.'
A poem either is or is not.
It can be about anything or nothing.
A blank wall or mirror would be
enough or too much for it. A dazzle.

AT THE GRAVE OF LITTLE FUCKER

Damnable cur,
I no longer hear your yap,
or see your matted fur.
You are under the mound.
A willow grows. No sound.

TO THE TURKISH LANGUAGE AND FOR KENNETH KOCH

You are always around me like a cloud,
a cloud shot through with sunlight,
but, like a cloud, I find you impossible to grasp.
O Turkish language, I want you to be luminous
and clear like sunlight, but solid like a handle!

PERFECT

In the transvestite bar
Padget turned to me and said:
'I've never seen so many perfect breasts',
and I said: 'Padget, they're not real',
and he said: 'I know but they're *still perfect*.'

TALKING TO THE LIVING

can be problematic.
There is the matter of disagreement,
but, as for the dead, if they are going
to answer back they have already done so.

ALEXANDER

And Alexander said that only sleep
and orgasm reminded him of his mortality.

So Persepolis burned,
and death came early in Babylon.

A jug of water killed him.

ALL PURPOSE ELEGY

O, it was here, but now it is gone!
It was always gone or going. It was here,
I am convinced of it, only a minute
or a century ago, and already I miss it.
Gone thing, will you come back, make
one last appearance, well-lighted like
a sunset over a lake between terrific mountains?

STOPPED

Everything stopped —
The clock, the fridge, the ancient stereo,
and finally the central heating.
Deep snow surrounded the house.
My father was dead. I put on his heavy coat.

SOUP

Ah Turkish soup
when all else fails there is you!

SUMMARY

O love, gloom, soup, language, music
people living, people dead,
hair, flowers, handsome waiters,
ruins and pollution, I am trying to love you all.
The alternative is eternal bitterness.

Part II

Basement Song

They have taken the beautiful perimeter
and covered it with sores with scabs

Their shit drifts out to sea —
history at best an ornament for the living room

elsewhere an impediment

For some the pool was enough
(winking blue idiotic)
even though the shrieks of children
covered it like an impenetrable net

the terraces were bleak as tundra
the flowers dead on arrival

they talked of absent enemies
gazed towards those broken pieces
of mountain half-drowned they called Europe

no escape from the school's black monuments —
black brow of the father bulging like a tumour

not wanting
not wanting to hear
the banal orchestrations of the town
pouring in like wet cement —

Towered over by a wall of old words
like sherds crushed under hideous sneakers
a peacock screamed by the café urinals

the music crashed like a train
the refugees in the dystopian hotel
had escaped from nothing worse than a bad smog
the corpses were put to bed still mumbling their orders
tribes cursed each other then danced under the uproar

O my tiredness
you were so all-inclusive like an opera
that I wanted only to fall asleep
with my hair in the ashes of the hearth

The empty vases remained in mind like a dado.

Where

What does it look like? Are the trees
strange, full of mechanical birds,
the arches askew and dipping down?
It is certainly a matter of place,
of finding. We have a world to live in,
which we should visit when time allows,
as during unforeseen and prolonged
periods of leisure like huge gold cushions,
perhaps after completing a book or a building
(since these are things we do, and do well,
until a doctor tells us we must stop,
and attend to the hammering of our nerves,
our hearts, which, as usual, are about to burst
in a shower of gulls or rain, and cover
the domes of the city with a black dust
which is impossible to interpret like a stone
inscribed with a dead, Anatolian language).

Some Places I Know and Do Not Know

I suppose I wanted to tell you about these places
because I find them beautiful and interesting,
but that looks too simple like a promise in an election year.
Some of them are interesting without being beautiful,
at least not in the sense that a head of Apollo is,
and there must be some places I know that are beautiful
in an uninteresting way; after all there are plenty of people
who fit this description: they are so physically perfect,
you have seen so many photographs of them
that when you finally encounter them you think:
'Yes, she, he or it is very beautiful, but I am bored.
They look like reproductions of themselves. They are
an outworn convention like naturalism in the theatre.'
And they often turn out to be a lot smaller than you expected.
Well, I have no intention of writing about such places,
but, in that case, which places should I write about?

I could tell you about my trip to *Albania*,
except that I have not yet been to *Albania*.
Some friends of mine recently went there,
and they are seasoned travellers, but I was worried —
it seemed to be a place from which everyone was fleeing,
so I rang another friend who had just been there, and he said:
'Oh, there's nothing to worry about. They have good
cappuccino.' He was in *Kazakhstan* at the time,
but he was right: the coffee was excellent,
and my friends enjoyed their visit, but then
they have a talent for enjoying themselves,
wherever they might happen to be. *Armenia*
is another place I am anxious to visit, and to that end
I have made a study of its history and geography.
Each year I promise myself I will go there,
but sadly you elude me, O land of the Hayk!

(for the Armenians do not call themselves Armenians)!
Georgia is one country I have been to.
On the main street of the capital city I met a man
dressed in an ankle-length floral frock and a straw hat
as if about to set out for a garden party,
but you could tell something wasn't working.

The guides were so desperate for you to like the place,
they were convinced in advance that you would not,
and presented you, at lunch time, with a cake
you could not eat. The museum lights were dim,
but I was able to see the jewelled cross of Queen Tamar,
whom all Georgians adore like an elder sister,
though she has been dead now for nearly seven hundred years.
There were emeralds, pearls and rubies. The whole effect
Was of elegant simplicity. (The Mongol invasions followed.)
I also liked the wine, the dumplings, and the churches,

and, in general, I have a great love of churches,
especially if they aren't Catholic or Protestant,
and ruined churches are best of all. It is like
the grand idea of God without god, abstract as a halo.
There is a place in Turkey called *Binbir Kilise*,
which means a thousand and one churches,
and there are a great many churches,
though nothing like one thousand and one of them
and some of them are very handsome, and seem to glow
like stupendous candles in the late afternoon light;
but others are nothing more than stones in a field,
and their glamour is only apparent in odd engravings.
It is certainly an interesting place, and beautiful,
but there are people have found it disappointing,
perhaps because they expected more churches,
or more complete churches, but when I am there
my heart is at peace amid the dry grasses,
and fruit trees grown wild. But I digress.

When I was a child, I often went
in summer with my family to The Borders,
where we would hide ourselves in the shadow
of the Black Mountains. I remember ruined abbeys,
tame birds, the bleeding hearts of peonies,
mumbling rivers, and I remember, though it cannot
be true, that the weather was always perfect.
High clouds rode by like regiments of an imperial
army that would harm no one. And I feel that,
in order to complete this poem successfully,
I should claim that these are the places that will
always be most deeply imprinted on my soul,
but I am not sure if it is true. I have seen
the *Lycian shore*, and the waterwheels of *Hama*,
and many wonders that the most shy and solitary child
could not imagine. O places I do not know,
and want to visit, I am on my way. *O Mush! O Yazd!*

The Long Poem

For some weeks now I have wanted to write a long poem,
but all I have produced are short poems, or poems
of moderate length, nothing that rolls on to the horizon,
and then plunges over it like a Niagara or an Iguassu.
Yes, it should be like a river! But where will I find its source?
In an idea or a word? Of course, it would be naïve
to assume that it has to be *about* something, but I fear
I have no talent for grand abstractions. Even the Parthenon
bores me: it is too perfectly Euclidean, if that is the right word.
So, long poem, when will you come, tripping along the street
    like
a beautiful girl in a red raincoat? You are surely a heartless
    lover.

Beds

1

The bed looks so inviting like a snowdrift
that all day long I have found it hard to resist.
Now night has fallen and it is raining,
and who knows what narratives await me!

2

The bed resembles nothing except a bed.
I can think of nothing to compare it to.
An iceberg? Oh, don't be silly . . .

3

The bed is empty and naked under the dirty windows.
It stands in a room that is also empty,
apart from itself, and an old wooden chest filled
with faded rugs of Anatolian workmanship.

The rugs are very lovely, and contain
three hundred years, but the bed cannot see them,
and knows its loss: 'O rugs, appear to me,
be my companions!' They will, they will.

4

The bed is warm and *dry*
in the sense of witty and ironic.

5

The bed lies under an attic roof
gazing blandly out to sea
as if it had a mind to become
a raft or a boat. This is hubris.

6

The bed is unhappy with its present living-quarters.
It can't stand the sight of the overdressed mirror,
or the bulging armoire. It looks as if it might rear up,
and canter away to find a better place to be a bed.
And where would that be? Sweden? Certainly,
it is utterly tired of nineteenth-century affectations.

7

The bed is in a relaxed mood,
neither too untidy, nor too rigidly composed.
Luckily, it is not of a military disposition.

8

The bed is a disaster!
It looks like a murder scene,
or the aftermath of angelic combat.
What have you been doing in it?

9

The bed detests hospitals,
where it is so weighed down with pain,
and painful recollection that it often
wishes it could turn into a block of wood.
It is not unsympathetic, of course,
but sometimes it whispers: 'Yes, yes I know

most of you must end here, but couldn't more of you
choose a hillside in spring, a sidewalk or a river?'

10

The bed is tired of sleep.
It throws the sheets into tantrums.
It keeps me awake all night
with its Procrustean strategies.
Bed, should I sing you a lullabye?

11

The bed proposes complex theories
concerning the hypnopompic state.
It wants to 'make something of itself', but what?

I think it should adopt a lighter approach.

12

The bed often reflects on The Great Beds of History —
the beds of Darius and of Alexander
who defeated him, the 'mattress grave' of Heine,
and the beds of all the great lovers. The bed
has visions of purple hangings, of gold, of shame
and happy lust, and is sometimes overcome with envy —
'Those beds really knew how to live!' And die, one might add.

13

The bed is in love, but not with me. The object
of its love is an unattainable ideal of obscure,
and fabulous origins. Splenetic humours
will be the result: breadcrumbs, spittle . . .

14

When the bed dreams, as sometimes it must,
it dreams it is an express train, or a flock of birds,
or a red sportscar driven by a laughing gigolo,
but, bed, in order to fulfil your destiny,
you must be still and silent, always silent.
Bed, I am sorry, but there is nothing I can do about this.

15

Bed, you are my first love,
I simply cannot live without you!
You are like air or water or a mother.

16

O go to sleep my bed.
Forget all the things I said,
And, dear, do not be led
Into the lands of the dead,
But sleep without dread.
Glide, bed, as on a sled.

To Music

On days when you give me no pleasure
I know I'm in trouble.

*

I know too much and too little
about you to say anything
definitive like the form of a sonata.

*

I love your diversity
like a display of vegetables
in an open-air market.
Motown? Mahler?
What exactly is the problem?

*

How many times would I have died
without you? You are simply
the sun, and most beautiful
when overcast.

*

When I am too calm, you excite me,
when I am too excited, you calm me —
not that I mistake you for a course of therapy.

*

There is no need to bitch
about the composers you don't like —
Tchaikovsky for example,
since you aren't obliged to listen to them.

*

The number of songs
is almost infinite.
I especially like the ones
about love and death,
then it is possible to cry,
and the day is over, whether
it has been good or bad.

*

I worry that I cannot read you,
that you are just air and vibrations,
but as essential to me as earth or stone.
I am desolate when I think of my ignorance,
yet you, it seems, forgive everything as
the late melodies of Schubert forgive everything.

*

But Schubert died of syphilis
after living for years with a drag-queen.
Chausson fell off his bike. Alkan
was crushed by a bookcase, and Berg
died of nothing more complex than a bee-sting.
Webern, we should remember, was shot
by an American soldier, and the soldier,
it turned out, was a lover of music,
and could not sleep once he knew what he had done.

*

Sadness surrounds music,
because it is temporal.
We know it will end, and we will
be expelled from that paradise,
and however much we repeat it,
like water, it cannot be grasped.

2 Miniatures

1. BITCHES

I like to think I give as good as I get.
He bitches me, I bitch him or her right back.
No problem. It is only after years of mutual
civility are reversed that I become disturbed.
Did I do that? Who was that person?

My behaviour, however bad,
is surely inconsequential. Who
would pay attention to it? I am
neither cathedral nor temple.

2. BASTARDS

Who is a bastard?
Anyone is a potential bastard,
but the real bastard knows nothing,
and will use this against you
like a mallet: he will slap your head.

You don't know this,
but you are some kind of statue,
and they want your pedestal.

Histories

In those days it was customary
for scholars to keep duplicates
of all their letters to fellow scholars or pupils,
then, in their declining years they would retire,
perhaps to an island, a mountain or a forest,
to write vast commentaries on their correspondence,
explaining in detail the aptness and elegance
of the many recondite allusions to ancient authors.

*

The kingdom of Rum lies so far to the west
that we possess very little reliable information
concerning it, but on certain facts there is general
agreement: the people there love to wear bright colours;
they travel everywhere in very fast conveyances,
and use heated footstools in the winter months. Also,
their ear-syringes are of superlative quality.

*

An anathema was pronounced,
then the anathema was anathematized.
A priest was flogged. Still the defeats continued.

*

The barbarians hammered at the gates.
Prince O was drunk, saying:
'Ha! What does it matter? Are we not
protected by the strongest walls in the empire —
walls in which we can clearly see,
in mortar and masonry, the accumulated

skill of centuries? Another drink my friends!'
and the city was utterly destroyed.

*

The king raged like a wild beast,
fell on the ground and ate dirt.
Hair sprouted from his back.
Only his sister could calm him, until
the saint was taken from the pit,
and the idols were broken. Then he smiled
and ate a dish of barley: this much
is a matter of record.

*

As he watched his palace burn,
how the minister lamented the loss
of the library, the art collection —
those bronzes of the best period,
their delicate eroticism . . .

But what of the servants
who had taken refuge in the cellars?

*

The walls were pulled down.
The altars were buried, and the town renamed.
A copse of fast-growing trees was planted
on the graves, but still the old people remembered,
and in the evenings, when memory must have its due,
they whispered their versions to grandchildren,
whose eyes grew wide with fear or understanding:

'In those days, this is how things happened.'
It was a sound like sand or shrivelled leaves.

*

His cloak was purple,
the purple of blood through which
he had waded to the throne,
but, against all odds, his reign
was prosperous, and the people loved him.
Provinces were reconquered;
palaces rose like dreams, but in his
last years he wanted nothing more
than to be reunited with his first-born son,
his beautiful son, who once rode into battle
at his side, clad in golden armour,
and had died suddenly of a fever.

A noted necromancer
arranged things for him, but the vision
melted away in his arms, and not long after
he met his end, and, like those of all his predecessors,
his corpse was exposed in the Hall of the Nineteen Couches.
O his lost son! He wanted nothing more.
He would have given up everything for that.

The Voices of Objects

Everything is speaking to us all the time.
We don't know this, but still they try to get through.
For example, did that chair give you permission to sit on it?
Did you even think of asking? I didn't think so.
It is time to consult your table's feelings. There it stands,
a fine and sturdy thing, and essential to your existence,
but so burdened with papers, buttons, pots, icons,
and uninterpretable souvenirs (there is even a spent
cartridge from the battlefields of Gallipoli
that a drunk gave you at a party) that it must surely
be deeply confused, if not in spiritual crisis.
At the very least, it must be wondering what kind of person
you are. You should wonder too. Perhaps this is what people
    mean
by 'The Wonder of Life', but I doubt it somehow.
But that objects have voices that haunt us is as certain
as the arrival of night. You have nothing to fear from either.

The Plumbers of Asia

O plumbers of Asia
how superior your work is
to that of the plumbers of Europe,

and yet, for some reason,
you are strangely denigrated.
The fine detail is ignored,
and it is very fine. There are, of course,
many varieties of plumbers
aside from the Asian and European,
and doubtless all have their virtues.
They migrate at different seasons,
and alight in different trees. In terms
of philosophy, aesthetics and mating habits
there are also very wide divergences,
so it is difficult to make confident
recommendations. Neo-traditionalists
are good if you want your waste-disposal
to have a late eighteenth-century feel.
Symbolists can be recommended
for those who require deep ambiguity
and a certain magnificent vagueness,
but an Expressionist would be sure
to make a mess of things, while neo-formalists
should be avoided at all cost: to correct
the situation a massive and expensive
wrench would be needed. In the end,

O plumbers of Asia,
it is your lyrical and improvisatory
compositions that most delight me,
filled with the sadness of flooded basements.

The Water
for Leyla

Though mentioned in no Chinese calendar,
it was the Year of the Water. It was running everywhere —
along streets, down the interior walls of apartments.
It was as if it had just discovered its character and fate,
and was filled with exuberance like children
just released from the care of a stern teacher,
but the water had its bad days. What was its purpose,
its plague or blessing? If it was dammed it was damned.
What was it to do? It should be free of course,
since it was in its nature to flow in any direction
it desired, yet it was not unreflective.
The water had been around for a long time,
and had been obliged to think about these matters,
even when it was evenly flowing in the manner
that seemed appropriate to it. Its freedom was important,
but it had no desire to drive people from their homes,
or drown the allegorical floor mosaics of Zeugma,
or require old women to sit in inflatable rafts.
While apologizing for its sometimes excessive enthusiasm,
the water felt misjudged and unfairly criticised, and said:
'I have nowhere to go unless our dialogue continues,
unless I can flood plains and retreat, and become docile
like a dog. But that I will never be. This is how
your civilisations came into being: growing populations
trying to control me produced agriculture and cities.
This is not a small achievement, so give me some credit,
and perhaps I will be kind, I the untameable
fresh water of rain and rivers, of lakes, waterfalls, rapids
taps, tarns, gutters and leaking downpipes! . . .
You have no way of knowing my moods, and yours confuse
    me.
I may choose not to turn your fields saline, but attend to me,

for I live in your house, even beside your bed. Attend,
for I may suddenly afflict you, and you will drown.'

Gormanzano

If there is a serious difficulty,
if, for example, you have no roof or water,
or you cannot finish your poem or painting,
you must call for Gormanzano,
and Gormanzano will laugh and say:
'I don't know, perhaps the flue is in the wrong place,
or the area of red in the lower left-hand corner
is too densely scumbled. It may also be the case
that your lover is entirely wrong for you,
but don't worry, I will find the workman
who can fix these things, and he will not be so
expensive. I will come tomorrow or the next day.'
And Gormanzano will come to inspect the details
of your difficulty, and he will laugh kindly,
causing you to feel that it is not such a complete
disaster after all, and you will not spend
the rest of your life staring at a damp wall,
or a wretched line of which you are ashamed.
Ah, Gormanzano, Gormanzano . . .

The Wait

The carpenter hasn't finished the closets.
The removal man can't find the address.
We are waiting in the coffee house by the Genoese tower.
No one appears, or at least no one we are waiting for.
The tall façades look dusty and faded.
A dishevelled poet with bad teeth sits at the next table.
He knows who I am, but is a man of tact and wit,
and doesn't try to show me his poems,
which, in any case, aren't available in English.
We continue to wait. We try the mobile and hear:
'The number you have dialled has not been assigned.'
Gülen is philosophical, and shows me her new pen,
which doubles as a cigarette lighter, but I am no good
at this sort of thing. Gülen is philosophical,
and Mel is, well, mellow, when not too melancholy,
but I am too often raging with impatience like a brush-fire,
and what, at the end of the day, is the real object of our
    waiting?
It cannot merely be the carpenter, even should he turn out
    to be
a religious leader of world-importance, which I
sincerely doubt. So what then? You can wait for anything —
a child, a woman, death, success, a Chinese
take-out, a drink, a bus or the Second Coming . . .
It is your choice what you wait for. But do not wait for love,
however you choose to define that elusive concept,
which people sing about constantly with such ecstatic
conviction. Personally, I would sing with more confidence
about a door, or the act of waiting outside a door.
But, assuming you are a mature adult,
love is a gift that you have already received
if it is ever going to come your way. If it didn't, it won't,
but it is possible that you failed to notice it: it was a letter

that looked so dull and official you threw it out
without opening it. That would be sad, but everything is
if that is your predisposition. After weeks of intense sunlight,
the sky is clouding over, and, above our heads, the vine is
    withering.
I order coffee. Gülen writes a letter to the carpenter. We sigh,
    and wait.

Part III

Everything . . .

Some nights I feel I can write about everything —
history, furniture, hydraulics, sex, the planet.
At other times my concerns seem absurdly narrow,
no wider than a crack in a glaze, and I feel I will
convince you of nothing, if convince is what I want to do,
like an expensive lawyer in front of a jury,

but metaphor is too easy: it proves
nothing, except that we require an answer
(a verdict), and will be endlessly cheated of it, like . . .

. . . and Nothing

It is what we look down into every day,
fighting the urge to let go of that chain
of associations (thorn to rose, elephant to cloud)
that attaches us to the habit of living. When
we consider what we can set against it, what virtue
or talent, a black hood descends. But we don't let go.

My Life

My life was ruined early, if at all,
but continues, though at some remove, now
that death has intervened like a cleaver,
conjuring madness, and a bag of bloodied clothes.

Father, sister, mother, I look at the phone —
black instrument — and my hand moves to dial
numbers that will connect something to nothing.
There is so much to be said that can never be said.

The mouth gapes. The face is frozen in the wrong position.

The Next Whisky Bar

When my father was dying,
he did a lot of travelling.
There were nights in the Tyrol,
days spent by the banks of the Rhone
or Rhine, and, for reasons we couldn't
fathom, frequent trips to Bristol.
Then there was the matter of his sight,
which had begun to betray him years before.
We didn't know what he was seeing,
so each day became a desperate act
of interpretation, but sometimes
the things he saw, or thought he saw,
made him almost happy for a time,
and, towards the end, he invented
an underworld that took the form
of a crowded bar or pub, located
directly below his hospital room.
It was entered by means of a long staircase,
and a narrow passageway, at the end of which
the doorman checked your papers carefully.
Once inside, there was singing and dancing,
and everyone drank 'good, Irish whisky'.
This was puzzling: he never drank whisky,
never frequented a pub. Even this phantasm
of the good life was not his, and soon
these inventions or borrowings failed him.
He became convinced that a key was lost
under his chair. Nothing more. Always the lost key.

Falling

When it snows in the city
I think of my gloved hand slipping
from the coffin I was helping to carry.
That night snow fell on my father's house,
on Manchester, on the river mouth
and the abandoned port. Annihilating
silence came down like a thick bolt
of coarse, grey cloth, horrible to wear,
and the only thing I could feel was the cold.
But in the morning the taxi arrived.
I caught the plane, and returned to my life.

It does not snow often in Istanbul,
but it snows sometimes. Then nothing moves,
talk slows, and everything assumes
an expression of blank amazement,
as if to say: 'This shouldn't be happening.'
Then you drink strong coffee without sugar.

Biography

Disconsolate, on that early August morning,
when first he heard the news, he may
have taken a walk in the park by the river,
looking for the last time at the things he loved.
According to meteorological records
it was raining, and it seems very likely
that he was carrying an umbrella,
but in the anguish of the moment
he may not have noticed the rain at all.

Perhaps he paused by a fountain,
in which case this must be the origin
of the sequence *Sad Fountains in the Rain*,
which remains his most popular work.
He would then have left the park by the east gate
(fixing its wrought iron in memory),
and have passed the portico of the museum,
where he had loitered so often as a child,
never daring to enter, before concluding his stroll
at his favourite café, *The Dead Pigeon*, of which
he speaks with such longing in his later work.

If we are correct in our assumptions,
it is virtually certain that he would have met there
with one or more of his closest friends —
Henry, Mehmet, Krikor or Old Max —
who would have offered him words of sympathy
on his great loss. He surely ordered a cognac.

Remembering Sex

Anything erotic is good by definition.
The ballet *Jeux* by Debussy is erotic,
erotic and mysterious, but sex now seems
to consist of unconvincing scenes
in movies of unsurpassed fatuity.
Even the hairstyles are an embarrassment.
Just when the dynamics of the plot
had begun to override your objections,
they undress and go to bed,
and their bodies are no longer handsome,
but products negotiating a merger.
By now we know more than we want to,
and they belong in a ruinous bathtub.

*

It is a common mistake to equate sex
with love, or at least to assume
that it is somehow 'meaningless'
without love, but sex always means something,
just as the words in a poem do, although,
in both cases, it can be hard to say what
that meaning is, and sex, to its credit,
is as unsentimental as a cat.

*

One sometimes hears people say:
'There is nothing wrong with sex
except for the trouble you have to go through
to get it.' It is usually a man who says this.
I cannot speak for women,
but sometimes their feelings cannot be so different.

It would be inhuman not to go crazy on occasion
over the cut of a thigh, and fuck the conversation
or the consequences. They are not paragons.

*

For some an element of risk
greatly enhances the experience of sex,
so, for example, they might choose to make love
in the path of a hurricane, on the slope of
an erupting volcano, on the roof of a house during
a flood or in a badly run game-reserve,
where, at any moment, they might be trampled
to death by a herd of wildebeest. It might be argued
that they would hear the herd coming
from a long way off, but in the throes of passion they
might not. Sliding off the roof could also be a problem,

assuming it was pitched.

*

Remembered sex is best.
Episodes in forgotten parts of Northern England
still haunt me. Who were these people?
They are old now, or perhaps no longer living
(and the bars are dark, the discotheques like tombs)
but I recall them in the moment of the thrill.
I remember their eyes, bright and devouring,
their prodigious cocks,
and none of them knew how absent I was.
It hardly seems to matter now. They were all
honourable in their way, and I remember them
like flares that burnt me a little.

*

You can have sex with anything —
a man, a woman, clouds, stars, landscapes
and architecture, but it is impossible to write about.
It is something you do without realising it.
Desire overwhelms you. You must go to that place,
meet that person, stand in amazement beneath
the dome of that building, or you feel you will die —
in the Elizabethan or Jacobean sense of dying —
if you do not immediately possess that rare tulip.

Imitation of the Virgin

After more than three years
of 'relative security' (unreal,
I never believed it) life has returned
to normal, that is to say, the rug has been removed,
the floor too. Once again, I resemble the Virgin Mary,
floating in mid-air with 'no visible means
of support'. Am I not saintly, female,
surrounded by stars and with child?

The broken books have lied:
sodomy is close to innocence, etc . . .
It only remains for me to found a religion,
and it had better be disgraceful, absurd:

otherwise, no takers.

What We Know

The brains of emperors have been dashed out
with soap-dishes. In such a world
how can anything be certain? One can say
'probably', as in: 'It was probably
in the reign of King Apranax the Atrocious
that a new form of mill-wheel was invented,
however, most people proved too superstitious
to use it.' And this, of course, is an example
I have just made up out of whole cloth.
Pride in knowledge, even if verifiable, is
an episode of ethnic cleansing, or
a sepulchre containing only a ratty broom,
some crushed beer cans, and a lemon rind.
As to which version seems best, *you choose*,
but the things we once thought we knew
are being reduced to paste or grape-jelly.

Sema

It is not always a matter of hands
fumbling under restaurant tables. Desire
is a much more difficult concept than sex,
and more expansive like a fertile steppe, yet
the two are closely linked in peoples' minds.
Desire is an essential part of sex, or ought to be,
but sex is not always a part of desire. For example,
it might be your passionate desire to visit Aleppo
or Hama, and eat the delicious falafel to be found
in those places, or, if you were a painter, it might be
a certain shade of blue that eludes you, and this blue
will be your firmament and fulfilment.
It will change tone and character with each hour
of the day, and by means of it you will become wealthy,
and move into an enormous loft, and very soon
the blue will drench everything you see,
and many other people will see it, and they will say:
'What do you mean, the kitchen furniture is white?
It is full of a mysterious blue that refreshes me,
and makes me want to create new things and travel
to new places that are beyond anything I imagined.'

In the end, desire is like hunger but more generous —
flourishing poplar at the end of an otherwise desolate valley.

Müze

In Istanbul there is a museum
of heating appliances
that I am anxious to visit,
but it is forever closed, and museums,
in general, disappoint me. I feel I am trapped
in a lecture-hall with the world's
most tedious scholar. Where
has the sky gone or the sun?
Ethnographic museums are the worst.
There are usually horrible mannequins
dressed in folk-costumes no sane person
would be seen dead in. I also have problems
with museums full of classical statuary —
all those marble buttocks and biceps,
and emperors got up in fancy armour, as if
they were on their way to a costume-ball
(and you know they've never seen
so much as a skirmish in their lives).

These things are old,
and have survived, which urges respect
but not idolatry, and after fifteen minutes
in the average museum I am overcome
with a desire to go out and sit in a garden
with living people. Only recall that the first building
to be called a museum was built in Alexandria.
Not a trace of it remains, and it was not a museum
in the sense that we understand the term.
Even its location is lost like a language
whose epic poems and grieving epitaphs
we can never know. Dead, nameless youth,
image of perfection, you are dust, close to nothing.

The Displeasure of Ruins

How must it feel to be exhumed
after centuries of living peacefully
under the earth, to be exposed to harsh sun,
blasted with rainstorms and penetrating cold,
to be patched up with cement, and
to be stared at by ignorant crowds
dressed in unsightly leisure-wear?

In Sardis there is grievance,
in Ephesus a chorus of angry complaints,
and at Sebaste the theatre is wounded
by the removal of its orange grove;
likewise the theatre of Nyssa mourns for
its uprooted olive trees, which gave it
such welcome shade. Sometimes the ruins
must dream of falling and crushing someone,

but they hold back: for our sake
they maintain an air of serenity
of damaged glory. Castrated Apollo.

The Place to Be

It is essential to really look at the place —
I mean the physical city or landscape
you live in, and consider whether it sometimes
inspires feelings of hope and desire, times
when the Platonic ideal of the right place appears,
splendid and ghostly, behind everything that is wrong,
for it is generally certain that a lot of things
will always be wrong. This clouds our vision,
but if you don't, on most days, love the place you live in,
as if it was the only place on earth, you had better get out,
otherwise you are probably dead without knowing it.

Nervous Poems

I climbed the steep street of music,
past ouds, and guitars, and gleaming pianos,
and I felt nervous.

I bought a newspaper,
and for no reason, felt nervous.

I went to lunch
but was too nervous to eat.
Why did the spinach taste of fish?

I returned to my apartment,
but was too nervous to stay there.
It was an obvious trap.

I walked down long flights of steps
but was so nervous I nearly fell.

I ordered tea in a favourite café,
but my nervousness made me spill it,
which embarrassed me, making me
still more nervous.

I walked to the harbour-front
to admire the view, but the screeching gulls
and the wet corpses on the fish stalls
only induced a new, more violent and ineluctable
form of nervousness. I fled by subway.

I talked to a friend,
but by now I was so nervous
I could barely hear him. He asked:
'Is anything the matter?' and I said
'Yes, but I don't know what.
It's like having a bomb in your heart,
and you don't know how to defuse it.'

I returned to my apartment once again,
and looked at my bed with longing,
but was much too nervous to lie on it.

I thought of playing music,
but the mere sight of all those hundreds
of recordings threw me into a panic.
They were all so different, how could I choose?

Then I thought of writing you,
nervous poems, and my hand moved freely.

Nervousness,
we cannot go on like this. But will.

Removed View

It is accomplished.
There is an end now, and a beginning.
The coloured chairs have settled in their corners,
the rugs from Van and the Caucasus
are on the floor of the corridor that otherwise
would seem too long — depressingly so —
like a sentence, and the lamps are lit,
the candles stowed away for emergencies. True,
the building opposite blocks the view,
but its baroque window-frames are handsome,
and women lower baskets from them so they can be filled
with bread or water, as their families require.
And I know the view is *there*, and, at night, gulls
drift above it like scraps of paper caught in the floodlights,
as if someone had torn up an unsatisfactory poem,
and however bad it may have been it was an attempt
to write the poem of this city, the poem that can be approached
but never reached. But now there is a beginning.

Returns

He tried to return, but the experiment failed.
Everything had changed. Old friends
had purchased houses in the suburbs,
which seemed to him like a life sentence.
But perhaps this was not the case. Perhaps
everything was too much the same,
and it was he who had been changed
beyond recall by the interval of exile,
as if the homeland were a winter coat
he was obliged to wear, made for someone
half his size. As was inevitable, the seams burst,
and he flew off, lost himself or found himself
in Galata's crooked streets, amid the spilt trash,
and stray cats, drank coffee under the gold point
of the tower. Sometimes going back is exile too.

Fasting, Not Sleeping

Along the street the shutters are being closed.
A metal drop, a dead sound as if the whole world
had been imprisoned, though it is only nightfall,
and the evening meal has been prepared, steam
rising from the soup, the fast ended for today.

It is the gathering at the midpoint,
and fireworks burst out of sight, above
the strait, the marble sea. Past midnight
children thunder overhead, as if playing
in a yard. Doors slam. Windows shake.

It grows quiet, until the drummer passes
in a riot of his own, chanting praises.
Then I hear my neighbours stirring,
their footsteps soft now, padded with sleep,
the sound dropping down to the foreigner below.

First light. Prayers done, the hunger begins again.

To the City

The village has come to the city.
In the narrow street, in the crowd
pressing down it, in the faces of tall buildings
we plainly see the shimmer of poplars
in the emptiness of the plateau, the huddle
of houses from which the voices of families,
and tribes before them, rise, reaching across
the sharp ridges of their displacement
to settle like smoke in the deepest hollows
of the city. They are near to us, in the store
or the next apartment, in the shadow of the tower,
yet are heard as distance, as ignorance,
and, in their echoes, the city seems to shudder
like something imagined from very far away —
glass city for those without windows. Their shoes
sit at doorways as if begging for admission.

Imprecation

The lost origins, the denied ancestors
have journeyed a long way in crowded buses
with vomiting children, only to stand
like beggars in a parking-lot, gazing up
at twenty levels of lighted windows
behind which the descendants are absorbed
in the polished machinations of a soap opera,
and do not hear their singing. They wait,
which is something they do well, but after a time
they grow angry, their voices whistle with malice:

'Look at the way these things are built!
Dried mud or dung would be better.
It will come down. It will all come down,
and the bridges will crack. It will be done
just as the Mother wishes, and she will wish it.'

Like statues, they don't go away.
They are here now, anger undiminished.
It will emerge, hissing, from your land-line,
or in cold sussurations at the edge of hearing.

Skiadion

How did it come about
that I boy from Manchester became obsessed,
at the age of thirteen, with the fate and reputation
of the Byzantine empire. I am convinced
there was something more to it than simple
eccentricity. My interest began with a question:
why had no one told me about this apparent gap
in space and time of over a thousand years —
a Roman breech, for they, the Byzantines,
never considered themselves anything but Roman,
their empire immutable, even as it shrank
and withered like an untended vine 'of formerly
vast extent', leaving on the last day, nothing
but a mutilated corpse, and a pair of purple boots
tangled in the aftermath of battle,
and a great cry of loss went up too late,
& the Venetians, who had done such damage,
did not set sail, and the Genoese 'observed
neutrality' — the West, as ever, craven,
unwilling to risk a life to save what it had ruined?
I was not too young to think this a vast injustice,
and I soon discovered that these emperors and stableboys,
princesses, and cleaners of monastic bath-houses
had been routinely slandered as 'decadent
and effeminate', the Roman grandeur brought low
by 'women and eunuchs'. I suppose their clothes
were wrong somehow, especially the magnificent
skiadion of Theodore Metochites,
and their literacy and cleanliness appalled
the barbarians (who we were). It was when I read
the words of Liutprand of Cremona, who dismissed them
as 'idle liars of neither gender', that I understood:
I *was* these people, and given the fact that I desired men,

equally slandered (this was some decades ago).
I called to my breast everything denigrated and neglected,
and was comforted. I travelled to the City, and sought
out the little that remained in shimmering fragments,
piercing together a homeland that was, and was not.
Under a hill the peacocks stood, opposed,
in their field of tall poppies (if they were poppies)
but the great urn they once reached towards was lost.

The City

It is the City, the only City.
Though it has many names, there is no need to name it.
It has existed since the seventh century BC,
when its citizens were renowned for their drunkenness,
but strangely no one now pays much attention to it,
even though it holds upwards of twelve million people,
who live on two continents, menaced by earthquakes.
On some days it is so crowded you can barely move.
Compared to it, Paris, for example is a suburb.

O City, City, eye of the universe,
ornament of the world, star shining afar —

your destiny is great, but your character
is sometimes hard to fathom, as if your entire mass
were below the soul's sea-level, and struggling to surface.
Dark City, City of inclines and islands, of channels and
    passages,

there are days when I don't know what to think of you,
you are so contradictory, so polymorphous
like a rapidly moving cloud-formation, but you command
my love like the place where I was born. You aren't perfect,
but perfection is not my goal, O difficult City,
under the storms of leaves and light! Promised to me —

Now

it is only a mound
with pine trees and beer cans,
now rubble, a column ensnared
by pomegranates
and tissue-paper flowers,
a house of brown fragments,
now waves wash over it,
and we look down to steps
and a cistern like a church,
now severe towers arise
with astonishing swiftness
then go out of fashion
(everyone hates them
as if they were a tyranny)
and the dust of their collapse
inflames the sunsets,

now the rich abandon
our district to gypsies,
now they begin to return,
as everything returns
like sand through a crevice,
then cafés flourish and close,
but others endure somehow
like olive trees in England,
now rats crowd in, or birds,
horsemen or trucks, and the sign
in the shabby hotel flashes:
'Invasions accommodated.
Varangians welcome',

now everything becomes a bank or mall,
and heads out into the landscape,
forming the nodes of an illuminated hairnet
covering the scalp of things we wish forgotten,

now headscarves come swarming
between the tenements,
and washing hangs like banners,
and now the gasman cometh
with his grievous refrain,
and, in recompense, every
family becomes an orchestra,
so that even the most noxious quarters
wax symphonic, lyrical . . .

now a looter's pit replaces
the tomb on the outskirts,
and doves dwell on window-sills,
and aqueducts are constructed
then cut, and floral fountains run dry
in the shadow of the planes
now it all begins to drift away —
out of sight, out of memory —
then it returns, all prodigal
and enthused in a bright, torn robe,

and we have a name for where we are,
but sometimes we don't know it,
or have to choose between confusing
variants in eroded languages, as if
permanently stalled at a crossroads,

and now the backdrops
to our opera-ballet, or opera-oratorio
fade and revive, recede and descend
like night, when the constant creaking

of the archaic mechanisms
that drive all of this lulls us to sleep,
and we dream we are somewhere else
that is similar in every detail except
that the forms have an exactness and rigour
unglimpsed in our waking hours, as if
moonlight had been sharpened to a blade —

in other words, no escape,
and no real desire to escape,
since it is certain that in time
we will be released like dust from a carpet
to which the maid has given her most
diligent attention, even though she arrived
out of breath at the top of the stairs,
smiling through broken teeth. Thwack!

Despite the Pontic cold,
Fatma has opened all the windows,
and, if the old edicts still apply,
from each of them we should look out
to a statue, a pillar or the sea,
but these things are often obscured
by fumes that attack the nostrils
like polished, bronze pins: then and
now we know where we are and when.